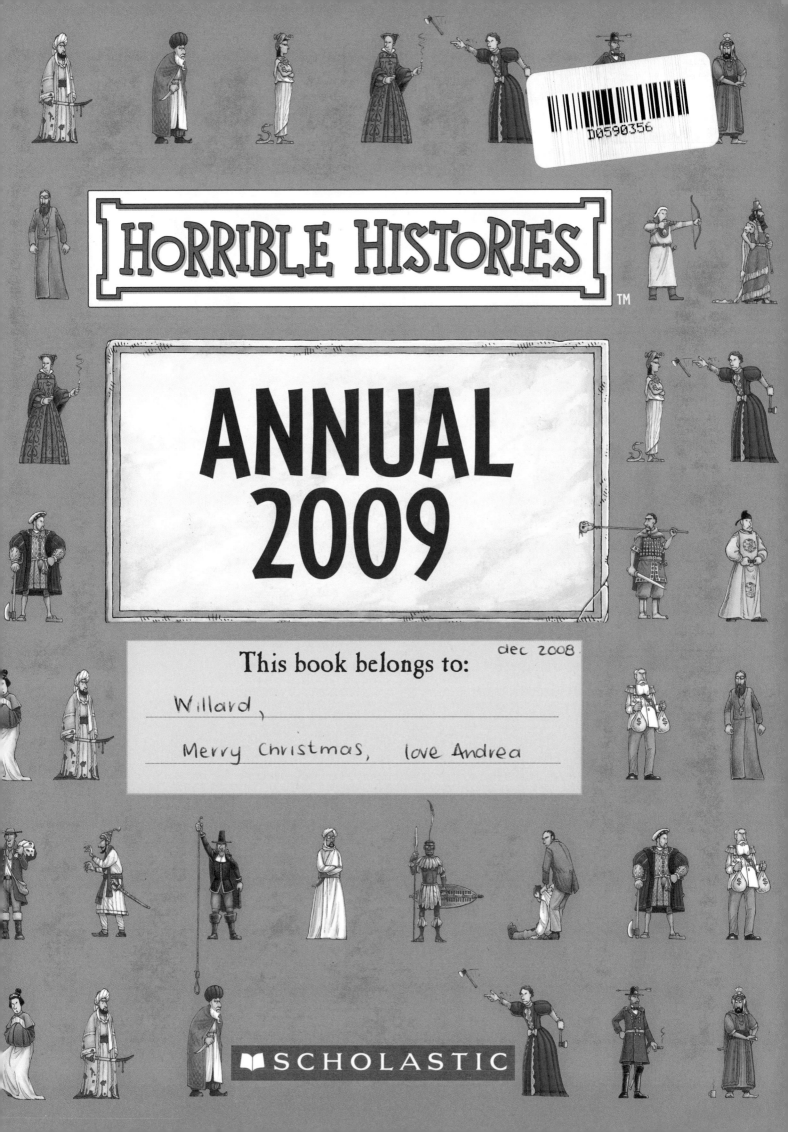

HORRIBLE HISTORIES™

ANNUAL 2009

This book belongs to: dec 2008

Willard,

Merry Christmas,   love Andrea

SCHOLASTIC

Contents

GOING UP
MODERN HUMANS
(THAT'S US!)
HUMAN-LIKE APES
HANDY MAN
UPRIGHT MAN
NEANDERTHALS
GOING DOWN

Awesome Ancient World

What a rotten place to be! Even in the 'civilized' world of the Greeks and Romans, punishments were painful, battles were beastly and the greatest game of all was watching people die...

HALL OF SHAME

ASHURNASIRPAL (C.883-859 BC)

THIS ASSYRIAN KING RULED HIS LANDS THROUGH TERROR. HIS ENEMIES WERE USED AS SLAVES – AND THEIR LEADERS WERE SKINNED ALIVE! THAT DOESN'T SOUND VERY A-PEELING!

ALEXANDER (356-323 BC)

ALEX WAS A MIGHTY CONQUEROR, BUT HE WAS ALSO A DEADLY DRUNK. HE CRUCIFIED HIS FOES, KILLED ONE OF HIS MATES IN A FIGHT – THEN DIED AFTER DRINKING TOO MUCH WINE!

CALIGULA (AD 12-41)

THIS ROTTEN ROMAN EMPEROR TRIED TO MAKE HIS HORSE INCITATUS INTO A CONSUL, THREW AUDIENCE MEMBERS TO THE LIONS IN THE CIRCUS, AND CLAIMED HE WAS A GOD!

BOUDICCA (AD 54-68)

BIG BAD BOSSY BOUDICCA WAS A FEARSOME CELTIC QUEEN. WHEN THE ROMANS TOOK HER LAND AND HAD HER WHIPPED, SHE SET OUT FOR REVENGE, BURNING ROMAN TOWNS AND BUTCHERING PRISONERS.

ATTILA THE HUN (AD 403-453)

AS KING OF THE HUNS, ATTILA SHARED POWER WITH HIS BROTHER – WHO HE LATER KILLED! ATTILA INVADED THE ROMAN EMPIRE AND BRUTALLY SLAUGHTERED ANYONE WHO GOT IN HIS WAY.

WORLD'S WORST EXITS

487 BC An entire Athenian army is wiped out in a battle against the Greeks of Aegina. The sole survivor staggers back to Athens to tell the soldiers' wives the terrible news. So what do the wailing widows do? They stab him to death with their brooches. What a point-less thing to do!

C.AD 50 A victim of a Celtic human sacrifice is hit on the head with an axe, strangled, has his throat cut, and is then thrown in a bog! (Talk about overkill!)

53 BC The Persians capture greedy Roman general Crassus. They killed him by pouring melted gold down his throat!

AD 260 Valerian, the Roman Emperor, is also grabbed by the Persians, who flay him alive (skin him).

BEASTLIEST BATTLES

1482 BC Megiddo – The Egyptians attack their Canaanite enemies in the fortress of Megiddo. The Egyptian soldiers hack off the right hand of each enemy's corpse to prove how many men they've massacred.

480 BC Thermopylae – Three hundred Spartan soldiers stupidly fight against tens of thousands of Persians. They know they don't have a chance. All 300 suicidal Spartans die. Still, everyone says they are very brave – dead brave, in fact.

Roamin' Britain

It took them a few goes, but when the Romans finally set foot on British soil, they changed the land for ever. Of course the Brits put up a bit of a fight – but the Empire struck back!

7

The Battling Brit

The Romans rampaged through Britain like bullies through a playground ... until they came up against a really tough cookie...

Big Queen Boudicca was a king-sized Celt with an attitude to match. When the Romans took her land, she led the Iceni tribe into the Roman town of Camulodunum (Colchester), burned it down, then torched Londinium (London) and Verulamium (St Albans) too.

Before this fiery rampage, there were several 'signs' that made people think that the gods were on her side. In Colchester, the Roman statue of Victory fell face down, as if it was surrendering. Women reported that ghostly, ghastly shrieks could be heard in the Roman senate house. At the mouth of the Thames, a phantom town was seen in ruins. The sea turned blood red and, as the tide went out, the sands took on the shapes of corpses.

HORROR OR HEROINE?

It's easy to imagine Boud as a true-Brit warrior heroine, but she wasn't actually very nice. As ever, there are two sides to every horrible history...

COWARDLY BOUDICCA ONLY ATTACKED UNDEFENDED TOWNS

THE ROMANS WRECKED THE UNDEFENDED BRITISH TEMPLES, SMARTY PANTS

THE BRUTAL BRITISH TORTURED PRISONERS, YOU BRAINLESS BRITON. BOUDICCA'S ARMY WOULD BURN, HANG AND EVEN CRUCIFY PRISONERS!

AND WHO TAUGHT US ABOUT CRUCIFIXION?

ER... THE ROMANS?

EXACTLY. SO WE WIN THE ARGUMENT!

AH, BUT WE WON THE BATTLE

DID YOU KNOW?

Boud's body is believed to be buried in London. But is it...
a) under her statue on Westminster Bridge (opposite the Houses of Parliament)?
b) under King's Cross Station?
c) at the bottom of the Thames?

(Answer on page 60)

King's Cross Station

MAYBE THEY SHOULD CALL IT QUEEN'S CROSS STATION INSTEAD!

A Soldier's Rotten Lot

It wasn't easy being in the Roman army – in fact it was stricter than school. But it was better than being one of the people you would bash, rob and trash!

When you joined the great army of the Roman Republic, you signed up for 25 years. But that wasn't so bad – you had wicked weapons, loyal colleagues and cunning commanders.

Tough stuff

But the Roman army's real secret weapon was – discipline. You know, the stuff your teacher says your class hasn't got enough of? Well, this army had more discipline than a dozen detentions. The soldiers did exactly what they were told every time. (They knew what was best for them.)

Company perks

Of course there were good bits to being a soldier too – otherwise no one would have wanted to join the army! The goodies included…

• **Plunder** You could make extra wealth by robbing the countries you defeated. You could take money, animals or even living prisoners who could be sold as slaves.

I THINK I'VE GOT THE SACK

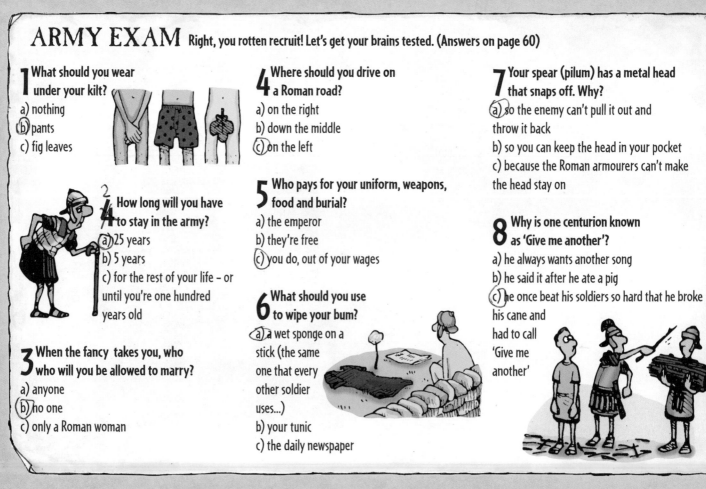

ARMY EXAM Right, you rotten recruit! Let's get your brains tested. (Answers on page 60)

1 What should you wear under your kilt?
a) nothing
b) pants
c) fig leaves

2 How long will you have to stay in the army?
a) 25 years
b) 5 years
c) for the rest of your life – or until you're one hundred years old

3 When the fancy takes you, who who will you be allowed to marry?
a) anyone
b) no one
c) only a Roman woman

4 Where should you drive on a Roman road?
a) on the right
b) down the middle
c) on the left

5 Who pays for your uniform, weapons, food and burial?
a) the emperor
b) they're free
c) you do, out of your wages

6 What should you use to wipe your bum?
a) a wet sponge on a stick (the same one that every other soldier uses…)
b) your tunic
c) the daily newspaper

7 Your spear (pilum) has a metal head that snaps off. Why?
a) so the enemy can't pull it out and throw it back
b) so you can keep the head in your pocket
c) because the Roman armourers can't make the head stay on

8 Why is one centurion known as 'Give me another'?
a) he always wants another song
b) he said it after he ate a pig
c) he once beat his soldiers so hard that he broke his cane and had to call 'Give me another'

• **Awards** There weren't any medals for brave actions – but there were three special crowns:

1) oak leaves – for saving the life of a fellow citizen (Julius Caesar won one for his part in ending the siege of Mytilene when he was just 20 years old)

2) plaited grass – for rescuing an army under siege

2) gold – for being the first soldier over the wall of an enemy town. (You'd better hope others followed you over – or you might not have a head to put it on.)

• **Pensions** The army took two parts of every seven you earned in wages and saved it for you. When you retired they gave you your

savings and some land. You could retire in comfort – if you were lucky enough still to be alive, that is!

Deadly docs

Roman army doctors knew how to…

BUT – Roman doctors didn't have anaesthetics to put you to sleep while they hacked you about! They would chop and knot, oblivious to the screams of the wounded man – not because they were deaf, but because they were trained to ignore them.

FASHION TO DYE FOR

If the Celtic warriors hadn't paid so much attention to their appearance, they might have stood a better chance!

• In battle, Celtic warriors often fought without any clothes at all. The Romans said that the Britons were painted from head to toe in a blue dye called woad … but maybe they were just blue with the cold! A bare blue Briton must have been pretty scary – but what would you rather wear? Roman armour or blue paint?

• Celtic men were proud of their hair. They bleached it by washing it in lime. The roots of the hair would be dark and the rest a bleached blond. The lime also made the hair stand on end. They went into battle with their hair in a crest of spikes. One writer said the spikes were so stiff and strong that you could have stuck an apple on the end of each point!
But this fierce fashion wasn't very clever. It meant they didn't wear helmets that could save their lives in battle – it would have spoiled their hairstyles!

... and now a baffling battle for your brains!

ODD GOD SHOW

Roll up, brainy bods! Can you spot any fakes among these Roman gods?

1 Cordia, goddess of hinges (she was a-door-ed!)

2 Robigus, god of mildew (that's mould on his robe I guess!)

3 Furrina, goddess of whatever you like – hamsters, holidays, ham sandwiches...

5 Penates, god of cupboards (what's he got in store?)

4 Terminus – god of boundaries (he really was the limit)

Latin Break

Seven Romans are hidden in the word square ... along with a beast that doesn't belong!

N	X	R	T	A	C	I	T	U	S
S	A	A	N	A	I	R	D	A	H
E	U	I	S	F	G	E	X	F	S
R	F	I	L	E	R	D	S	A	X
V	E	A	N	L	I	O	R	S	R
I	L	J	P	O	U	H	I	B	D
A	K	R	W	Q	T	T	V	U	D
N	M	Z	U	Y	H	E	R	C	S
U	B	O	M	N	G	B	U	E	A
S	U	I	D	U	A	L	C	S	T

TACITUS
SUETONIUS
HADRIAN
CLAUDIUS
MITHRAS
DIO
TERTULLIAN
SERVIANUS

ICENI SCENE

Run for your lives – the Iceni are going crazy in Camulodunum! Can you see six differences between the pictures?

Answers on page 60

12

Monstrous Middle Ages

Welcome to the Middle Ages – when Vikings came to slash and slay, and stormin' Normans came to stay. It was a time of nasty knights and crazy crusades.

HALL OF SHAME

ERIK BLOODAXE (928-933)

THIS VICIOUS VIKING KILLED SEVEN OF HIS BROTHERS, SO HE COULD BECOME KING OF NORWAY. BUT HIS ROTTEN REIGN ENDED WHEN HE WAS AMBUSHED AND KILLED BY HIS ENEMIES. SERVES HIM RIGHT!

KING WILLIAM I (1066-1087)

WHEN WILLIAM ATTACKED THE FRENCH TOWN OF ALENCON, THE DEFENDERS MADE FUN OF HIM. SO HE CAPTURED 31 OF THE TOWNSFOLK AND HAD THEIR HANDS AND FEET CUT OFF. AND THAT'S NO JOKE!

GENGHIS KHAN (1165-1207)

GENGHIS KHAN WAS A MEAN MONGOL CONQUEROR. ONCE HE ORDERED HIS MEN TO CUT OPEN SOME PRISONERS' BELLIES – TO SEE IF THEY HAD HIDDEN THEIR JEWELS BY SWALLOWING THEM.

KING JOHN (1199-1216)

JOHN WAS REALLY ROTTEN. DURING A REBELLION IN FRANCE, HE CAPTURED OVER 200 KNIGHTS AND TREATED THEM SO CRUELLY THAT 22 OF THEM DIED. HE DIED BECAUSE HE PIGGED OUT ON PEACHES AND CIDER.

KING RICHARD III (1483-1485)

ROTTEN RICHARD DID DOZENS OF DASTARDLY DEEDS. SOME SAY HE HAD HIS TWO LITTLE NEPHEWS MURDERED IN THE TOWER OF LONDON SO THAT HE COULD BECOME KING OF ENGLAND.

WORLD'S WORST EXITS

1327 King Edward II is thrown into prison by his wife, and then murdered. It is a nasty way to go ... his killers push a red-hot poker up his bottom.

1333 In Japan, almost all of the Hojo family of Samurai commit suicide in a cave because they are about to lose a battle. Hojo Takatoki begins by cutting open his own belly and pulling out his guts. About 870 others follow his example.

1358 When Will Cale leads a peasant rebellion in France in 1358, he is captured and crowned – with a red-hot crown. Then his head is cut off and stuck on a stake.

1421 Joan of Arc is accused of witchcraft ... and burned alive at the stake.

BEASTLIEST BATTLES

1066 Hastings – King Harold is exhausted after beating his brother, Tostig, in northern England. But with no time to rest, he marches south to fight the Normans. Harold cops an arrow in the eye – a sore-eye day for the English!

1415 Agincourt – The English beat the French by hammering wooden stakes in the ground to trip up the enemy horses. The French knights, in heavy armour, drown in the mud or get shot by longbow arrows.

EYE DIDN'T SEE THAT COMING

Frights in Armour

Here's how The Middle Ages became an absolute knight-mare!
It's a story of castles, crosses and terrible losses...

16

Little Villeins

The Normans ran their countries under a 'feudal system'. Imagine it as a pyramid...

GOSH! IT'S A LONG WAY UP!

The king sits at the top and owns the lot.

The barons guard the king's land and train the men to fight for the king who sits at the top and owns the lot.

HMM, NICE VIEW!

The knights look after the villages and fight for the barons who guard the king's land and train the men to fight for the king who sits at the top and owns the lot.

The villeins work on the land and work for the knights who look after the villages and fight for the barons who guard the king's land and train the men to fight for the king who sits at the top and owns the lot.

WHERE WOULD FEUDAL EXPLANATIONS BE WITHOUT PYRAMIDS?

WHERE'S THE GRATITUDE?

The serfs belong to the land (whoever is in charge) which is looked after by the knights who look after the villages and fight for the barons who guard the king's land and train the men to fight for the king who sits at the top and owns the lot.

TEST YOUR METAL

There's more to being a knight than prancing around with a lance, you know. Can you pass this exam in nasty knighthood?

1) King Edward I of England has set up a tournament and he will be fighting in it. What do you do?
   a) Fight in the tournament to the death – even if it means killing the king.
   b) Fight with a special sword that won't harm anyone too much.
   c) Refuse to fight.

2) What is a 'knight errant'?
   a) A knight who wanders around Europe looking for good causes.
   b) A knight who has failed in battle and is a disgrace.
   c) A knight who makes lots of errors.

(Answer on page 60)

3) You are a knight captured in battle by a squire. This is a disgrace because he's not a knight! What do you to him?
   a) Make him promise not to tell.
   b) Make him into a knight.
   c) Kill him and keep quiet about it.

4) You capture an opposing knight in battle. He is rich. What do you do?
   a) Kill him and steal anything valuable on his body.
   b) Kill him, then send his body and all his belongings home to his family in a horsebox.
   c) Let him live then sell him back to his family for a small fortune.

Bad Manors

Norman barons took English land as their 'manors'. They made the locals work hard and pay taxes too. No wonder the barons lived behind fierce fences!

MOUND OF TROUBLE

1. The poorest peasants were called serfs – and they had almost nothing.
2. Peasants prided themselves on keeping their houses clean. They really gave dirt the brush-off.
3. As if their lives weren't wretched enough already, the serfs had to give one tenth of their crops to the church. Holy unfair!
4. Pigs were taken to the forest to feed. They weren't easy to control…
5. The bailiff was the Norman baron's top chap – so people hated him!
6. A Norman baron lived in a 'motte and bailey' – an early type of castle, surrounded by a wall of sharp stakes called a 'palisade'.
7. Only barons and their knights were rich enough to own horses.
8. Each manor had a blacksmith to make horseshoes and swords and to mend tools. In fact, he could 'iron' out most problems.
9. The baron could stand on his motte (a high mound) and look over his manor as if it were a little kingdom.

Joustin' Time

Tournaments were 'joust' the thing in the Middle Ages.
Nobles and peasants would turn up to see knights charge
at each other. Thrills and spills were guaranteed!

JOUSTS
ARE
JUST EVIL

A LETHAL LANCE-A-LOT

1. Crafty knights had themselves bolted into their saddles so that they couldn't fall off in a joust.
2. The winner of a joust got to keep his opponent's armour. Suit's yours, Sire!
3. The herald was like a Middle Ages sports commentator – he knew the scores!
4. A knight got points for knocking an opponent off his horse – or for breaking his own lance! How shattering.
5. Knights could fight on foot, too. There were lots of ways they could beat each other's brains out in this 'knockout' competition.
6. Some helmets gave very good protection against lances – but were almost impossible to see out of!
7. Peasants weren't allowed to joust, but they could join archery contests. They fired arrows at targets called 'butts'… not that kind!
8. Getting your squires to bash an opponent before a joust was cheating, but it helped you win!

... a lance chance brain tournament!

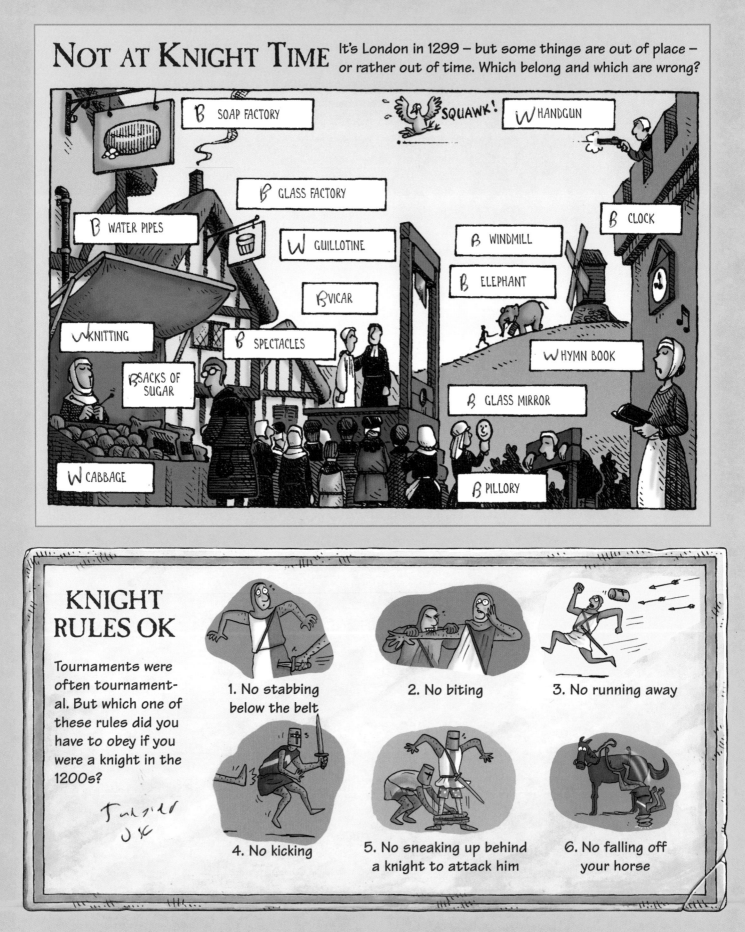

NOT AT KNIGHT TIME

It's London in 1299 – but some things are out of place – or rather out of time. Which belong and which are wrong?

B SOAP FACTORY
SQUAWK!
W HANDGUN
B GLASS FACTORY
B WATER PIPES
B CLOCK
W GUILLOTINE
B WINDMILL
B VICAR
B ELEPHANT
W KNITTING
B SPECTACLES
W HYMN BOOK
B SACKS OF SUGAR
B GLASS MIRROR
W CABBAGE
B PILLORY

KNIGHT RULES OK

Tournaments were often tournament-al. But which one of these rules did you have to obey if you were a knight in the 1200s?

1. No stabbing below the belt

2. No biting

3. No running away

4. No kicking

5. No sneaking up behind a knight to attack him

6. No falling off your horse

22

Answers on page 60

GOING UP
EXPLORERS IN NEW WORLDS
CRICKET BALLS
POTATOES – CHIPPED, MASHED,
BOILED OR ROASTED
THE SPANISH ARMADA
MARY QUEEN OF SCOTS ...
HER EXECUTIONER'S AXE
GOING DOWN

Sinister 16th Century

The 1500s were brutal and beastly. Savage explorers roamed distant lands and ancient empires made desperate last stands. And, of course, there was no one ruder than a terrible Tudor!

HALL OF SHAME

FRANCISCO PIZARRO (1475-1541)

THIS SPANISH EXPLORER WAS AN EX–PIG–HERDER WHO PULLED OFF THE BIGGEST ROBBERY IN HISTORY. HE CONQUERED MILLIONS OF INCAS WITH AN ARMY OF 260 MEN AND STOLE 6,017 KILOS OF GOLD.

HENRY VIII (1491-1547)

SERIAL ROMANCER HENRY WAS A MEAN KING WHO HAD A TERRIBLE TENDENCY TO EXECUTE ANYONE WHO DISPLEASED HIM – AND THAT INCLUDED TWO OF HIS SIX WIVES WHO ENDED UP LOSING THEIR HEADS.

IVAN THE TERRIBLE (1533-1584)

IVAN WAS A CRAZY RULER OF RUSSIA WHO HAD A MURDEROUS SENSE OF HUMOUR. HE ONCE HAD AN ARCHBISHOP SEWN INTO A BEAR'S SKIN AND THEN HAD HIM HUNTED DOWN WITH HOUNDS.

MARY I (1516-1558)

THIS MISERABLE QUEEN HAD NO SENSE OF HUMOUR AT ALL. SHE TOOK HER RELIGION SO SERIOUSLY THAT ANYONE WHO DIDN'T SHARE HER BELIEFS WOULD END UP SIZZLED AT THE STAKE.

ELIZABETH I (1533-1603)

'BAD BESS' WAS AN OUTRAGEOUS FLIRT WHO LIKED TO GO AROUND COURT WITH HER TOP OPEN. SHE'D SLAP ANY GIRL WHO WAS GETTING TOO MUCH ATTENTION, AND ALSO GAVE AN EX–BOYFRIEND THE CHOP.

WORLD'S WORST EXITS

1528 Italian explorer Giovanni da Verrazzano lands on a Caribbean island and is met by a bunch of cannibals. They grill him and eat him for tea.

c.1560s Ivan the Terrible is so irritated by one of his guests that he pours boiling soup over him. When the guest screams, Ivan stabs him to death. Later Ivan attacks another man and cuts off his ears. Perhaps he is ear-ritated.

1572 At the St Bartholomew's Day Massacre in Paris, Admiral De Coligny is dragged from his bed and stabbed in the belly till his guts fall out. Still alive, he is thrown from a high window into the street. His fall is broken by the pavement ... Splat!

1587 As Mary Queen of Scots is executed the axeman's first chop misses her neck and hits her head. His second shot is a bit better but he still needs a bit of sawing to hack the head off.

BEASTLIEST BATTLES

1578 Battle of the Three kings – King Sebastian of Portugal and two Moorish kings fight it out in North Africa – but all three rulers are killed!

1588 Defeat of Spanish Armada – A Spanish fleet sets out to conquer England, and it seems nothing can stop it. The Spanish ships are harder to sink than the English expected. But bad English weather comes to the rescue. Storms drive the Spanish ships all over the place – many are sunk and England is saved.

Simply the Bess!

From her flame-red wigs to her Tudor toes, she was bossy to buddies and fouler to foes. So bow down to Elizabeth the First ... or fear the worst!

The English loved Elizabeth. She was a fashion icon and a real 17th-century celebrity.

'Good Queen Bess' was also known as the Virgin Queen, because she never married. But Bess liked to flirt. She once had a meeting with an official with her gown open to the waist! Even if she didn't always button them up, Bess loved her dresses … all 3,000 of them.

Poisonous Profile

Name: Elizabeth Tudor (also called Good Queen Bess, Eliza, Gloriana, the Virgin Queen)

Born: 7 September 1533

Mum and Dad: Henry VIII and Anne Boleyn

Religion: Protestant

Husband: Not likely!

Reigned: 44 years and 4 months (17 November 1558 until her death)

Died: 24 March 1603

Tudor temper

As she got older and wrinklier, Bess grew jealous of pretty women. She slapped one, Lettice Knollys, for looking attractive (and also for secretly marrying Bess's old boyfriend).

And if someone tall annoyed her she promised to make them "shorter by a head". She had her taller cousin Mary Queen of Scots cut down to size – not for being tall, but for plotting against her.

In fact, lots of people wanted Bess dead. (She'd once been put in the Tower by her sister, Mary!) But Bess was more than a match for them. After crushing a Catholic uprising in 1569, Bess had 450 rebels sliced open while they were still alive. In later years Bess took to carrying a rusty old sword around her palace in case she was attacked.

 HORRIBLE HAPPENINGS

HANDS OFF BESS

John Stubbs wrote a rude leaflet about one of Bess's boyfriends. So Bess had his hand chopped off with a butcher's knife. Before he fainted, Stubbs used his other hand to wave his hat and cry, "God save the Queen!" The message was: don't be rude about royals!

THOSE WERE THE DAYS

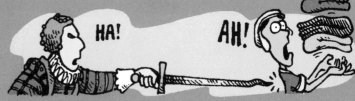

HA! AH!

Good clean Bess

Bess liked to wash. A writer noted that she had a bath every three months "whether she needed it or not".

She did, however, have horrid blackened teeth because she ate so much sugar.

Beauty Queens

Bess was so glamorous that everyone copied her look. Even the men! But being a fashionable Tudor could mean following some truly vile styles.

Poor Tudor folk itched in their rough woollens, while the rich dressed like supermodels. Merchants brought lace, velvets, satins and starch from overseas. Starch meant they could make trendy stiff collars called 'ruffs'. But were they…

RUFF OR DUFF?

• Sometimes the stiff ruffs were so wide that ladies couldn't reach their mouths to eat! Extra-long spoons had to be made.

• Ruffs were usually white, but could be any colour. Yellow was 'in' for a while – but then a famous murderess, Mrs Turner, was hanged wearing one. Yellow ruffs suddenly went out!

• Elizabethan men wore short trousers called 'hose'. To hide their puny legs they padded them with rags, horsehair or even bran!

• Poor country girls often wore shoes with iron rings under them. Sometimes they had thick wooden soles. This was to keep their skirts out of the deep mud and poo in the streets.

• The Elizabethan ladies' fashion was for tiny waists. To help them squeeze into smart dresses, the ladies – and even the girls – wore iron corsets.

To be the Bess

To look like the queen you need…

HIGH FOREHEAD
RED HAIR
PALE SKIN
RUBY LIPS

• Make skin paler with lead paint (lead is deadly, by the way), vinegar, egg white and poppy seeds.
• Paint your lips with paste made from cochineal and more egg white. (Cochineal is a red dye made from crushed beetles. So put a bug on your mug!)
• Pluck hair for a high forehead, then dye what's left with sulphur. Soon your hair will fall out, so…

Wear a wig. Bess had about 80 of them! Men dyed their beards red and tamed them with sticky wax. At night they held the beard in shape by popping it in a special teeny chin-cap or a clamp.

If you smell … don't wash. It's not healthy. Cover your pong with perfume. Go on, chuck on more. Now you really look and smell like a terrible Tudor!

JUST THE SMALL BOTTLE OF PERFUME THEN IS IT MISS?

Acting Up!

"All the world's a stage," wrote Shakespeare – and his plays certainly left nothing out! For a round helping of rudeness and gore, come on down to London's Globe Theatre...

STOP! FUN IS EVIL

THE GOOD GLOBE GUIDE

1. The Globe was shaped like an enormous ring doughnut, with the stage and an open 'Pit' area in the middle. Posh folks (1A) paid two pennies to stand in the sheltered galleries around the ring. It cost extra to park your bum on a cushion (1B)!

2. Poorer folks paid just a penny and stood in the open Pit. These spectators were known as 'groundlings' and kept things lively by shoving, yelling, throwing up and arguing with the actors.

3. Puritans and other religious spoilsports reckoned the theatre was evil and should be banned. They said plays were full of bad language, violence and rude acts. And they were right!

4. On stage is a performance of *A Midsummer Night's Dream* by William Shakespeare. It features romance, rude jokes, fairies and a donkey-headed chap called Bottom!

5. The very rich watched from chairs on the sides of the stage – within spitting distance of the actors. (That's 'saliva'-ly place to sit!)

6. Actors playing angels or fairies 'flew' by swinging around on ropes let down from the 'Heavens' – the painted ceiling over the stage.

7. To let the public know that a play was about to start, the theatre owners fired a cannon. But cannons and wooden buildings don't mix. In 1613 a cannon blast set fire to the theatre roof – and the Globe burned down. (It was re-built immediately.)

8. People in the streets could work out what kind of play was on by looking at the flag on the theatre's flagpole – black for terrible tragedy, white for chucklesome comedy, or red for horrible history!

9. These 'actresses' getting ready for the stage ain't no ladies! It was against the law for women to act, so female roles were played by teenage boys in dresses.

10. When he wasn't busy scribbling more plays, Shakespeare himself sometimes appeared in his own productions. He played minor characters like guards and servants.

Hello Sailor!

Good old Bess loved nothing more than a sailor and sea-faring Sir Francis Drake was a favourite. He sailed the world raiding Spanish ships and gave her the loot. What's not like?

In 1588, fed up with being robbed and cross that Bess had given her Catholic cousin the chop, the king of Spain sent a fleet of warships (the Armada) to battle it out with the Brits.

It was Sir Francis Drake's job to fight off the Armada, but he spent his time trying to nab the pay ship and grab the gold

Dirty trick

As well as being greedy, Drake could also be cruel. Once he captured a Spanish ship. Most of its crew had jumped and swum ashore, but Drake took a captive. Drake wanted to find the ship's loot. So he threw a rope over a rail, tied the other end round the sailor's neck, and pushed…

A-MAZING ARMADA

Drake didn't have to do much fighting as the bad weather did it for him. Can you help the Spanish ships find a safe route through the gaps in the waves without getting sunk?
(Answer on page 61)

The rope hadn't been tied to the rail, so the man hit the water unhurt – but terrified. Back on board he soon blabbed to Drake!

Scary 17th Century

GOING UP

ENGLISH TAXES
PLAGUE
LONDON (IN FLAMES)
THE SLAVE TRADE
HAVING A GOOD TIME
WITCHES
GUY FAWKES
THE EXECUTIONER'S AXE

GOING DOWN

In Britain there was a savage civil war and the Stuarts made Charlies of themselves. In the Americas it was unsettling to be a settler – and lethal to be a local!

HALL OF SHAME

JAMES I (1566-1625)	OLIVER CROMWELL (1599-1658)	CHARLES I (1600-1649)	GEORGE JEFFREYS (1648-1689)	AURANGZEB (1618-1707)
THIS DRIBBLING KING HAD FILTHY MANNERS, AND HE LOVED TO PICK HIS NOSE (GROSS) HE ALSO LIKED PICKING ON CATHOLICS AND HAD MANY OF THEM TORTURED AND PUT TO DEATH (GRUESOME).	THIS WARTY WARRIOR THOUGHT HE WAS GOD'S GIFT TO THE ENGLISH – SO AFTER HE WAS DEAD AND BURIED, HIS BODY WAS DUG UP AND. PEOPLE TORE OFF BITS AND PIECES TO KEEP OR SELL AS SOUVENIRS.	THIS MINI-MONARCH WAS SHORT ON INCHES (HE WAS EVEN SHORTER AFTER HE GOT THE CHOP!) – AND ON LAUGHS. CHARMLESS CHARLIE WAS SNOOTY, STUPID AND SPOKE WITH A SQUEAK.	DREADFUL JUDGE JEFF LOVED SENDING REBELS TO THEIR DEATH IN REALLY HORRIBLE WAYS. AND IF HE COULDN'T HAVE THEM KILLED AND CHOPPED UP, HE'D HAVE THEM FLOGGED OR SENT OFF TO COLONIES.	THIS MEAN MUGHAL RULER OF INDIA WAS A BIT OF A MONSTER. HE HAD HIS BROTHERS BEHEADED, HE LOCKED HIS DAD IN A PRISON – AND THEN HE DECLARED HIMSELF 'WORLD CONQUEROR'.

WORLD'S WORST EXITS

1649 Charles I is beheaded on Oliver Cromwell's orders. His head is then sewn back onto his body so his family can pay their respects.

1649 Royalist rotter Sir Arthur Aston is battered to death at Drogheda in Ireland. His killer uses the first weapon he can find, which is Sir Arthur's own wooden leg!

1658 When Oliver Cromwell dies, royalist soldiers drag his rotting body from its tomb and take it down to the pub for a drink. After this, they hang it on the public gallows, rip the head off and stick it on a spike on top of Westminster Hall – for 24 years!

THERE'S A THUMB IN MY RUM

1676 Indian chief King Philip is killed in an ambush and hacked to pieces. His hand is given to his killer, who pickles it in rum!

BEASTLIEST BATTLES

1622 Jamestown Massacre – Indian Chief Opechancanough sends out a 'peace party' to talk to settlers. After sharing a hearty breakfast, his warriors slaughter 347 of them. Twenty-two years later, the cheeky chief plays exactly the same trick again ... and kills 300.

SOME PEOPLE NEVER LEARN

THE WORDS 'SOME PEOPLE NEVER LEARN' COME TO MIND

1642 Edgehill – In England, Royalists and the Roundheads get into a muddle in the first major battle of the Civil War. Both sides claim to win, but really it's a dreadful draw.

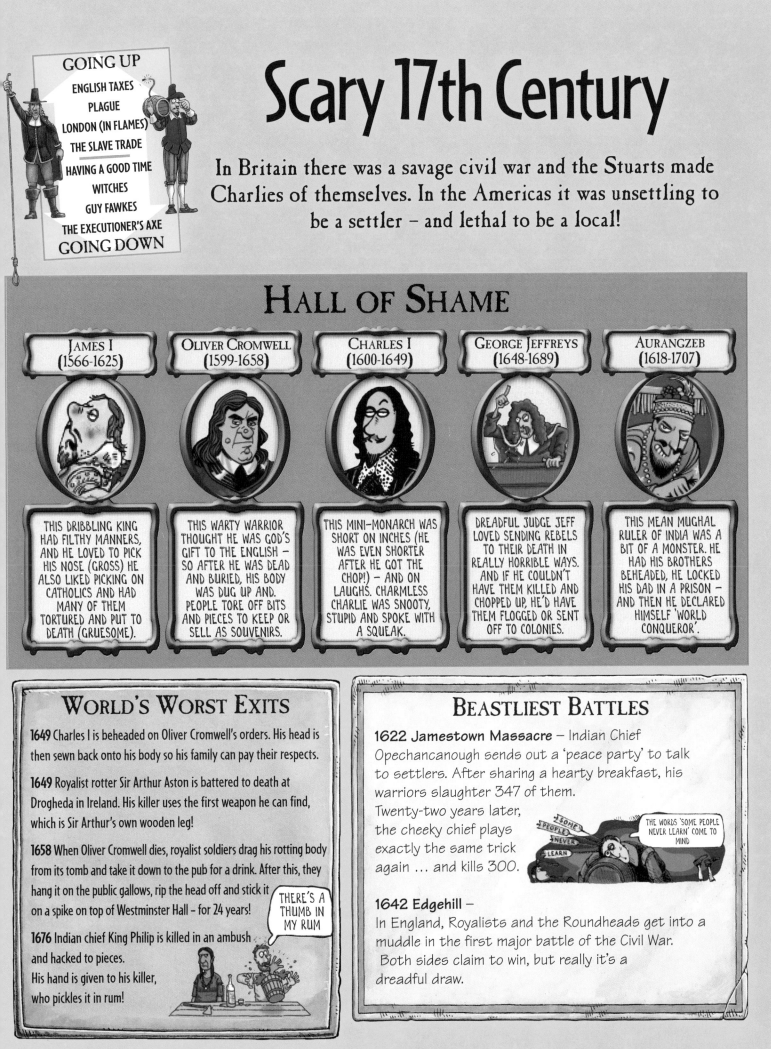

32

... and now for some punishing puzzles

PURITAN PUNISHMENTS

The Puritans brought in niggling new laws after they won the Civil War.
Can you match the rotten wrongdoing with its Puritan punishment?

CRIME

1) Disagreeing with the Puritan religion

2) Trimming a beard on a Sunday

3) Stealing lead from a house roof

4) Performing in a Shakespeare comedy

5) Going to church on Christmas Day

PUNISHMENT

a) Fined

b) Having your orchard dug up

c) Being whipped for two whole hours

d) Getting sent to prison

e) Time in the stocks with Puritan poetry around your neck

NECK NICK-NACK

Long after Charles I died, a repulsive royal doctor stole a neck bone from his corpse... and put it to a tasteless new use. What was it?

A) Pastry cutter

B) Salt cellar

C) Baby's dummy

D) Stethoscope

(Answers on page 61)

Sick City Scene

In 1665, the plague spread across England like boils on a victim's body. London was the zittiest city – over 100,000 people died here. It was a case of flee from the fleas – or die of disease!

Nurses hired to care for plague victims weren't always nice. Helpless plague patients' property was easy pickings!

The Stuarts didn't know it, but the plague germ was carried around by rats' fleas. Two-thirds of those bitten by the beastly bugs died.

The plague gave you lumpy 'buboes' (swellings like boils) on your armpits, neck and groin – plus vomiting, achy limbs, fever and finally death.

IT'S ENOUGH TO BRING A LUMP TO YOUR THROAT!

Red crosses painted on plague victims' doors warned healthy people to stay away. (Maybe they used Xs because the occupants were soon to be 'X(ex)-people'?)

Doctors thought the plague travelled in 'foul air', so they wore special masks. What airheads! Their costumes were enough to scare you to death.

Fires were lit to 'sme out' the plague. This wasn't such a hot ide it just choked people

Poor pussycats copped it! Pets were mistakenly blamed for spreading the plague. Bet the rats were pleased!

Muddled Medicine

The poor old Stuart doctors had no idea what caused the plague or how to avoid it – in fact, they didn't know much about saving lives at all.

It's no wonder all those people died of the plague as doctors thought that pets, pigs and pigeons were spreading it. So after 120,000 cats and dogs were killed in London alone, there were none left to catch the real culprits – the rats.

Other doctors blamed dirty air, so huge bonfires were lit in the hope that they would 'purify' it. Some people thought God was punishing them for their sins – so they went to church.

AH, THAT'S MUCH BETTER, NICE PURE AIR

Quacks in Beaks

Desperate doctors tried to keep out the plague with this kooky kit. Did it work? Not a bit!

The birdlike beak was stuffed with smelly herbs to banish 'bad air', while the hat and mask kept the head completely covered. All useless – but they made the docs look terrifying!

A big stick was useful for beating off plague victims who got too close. Who wants to come to a 'sticky' end?

Each doc wore a cloak that was waxed to make it shiny, so that plaguey air couldn't stick to it. That was utter rubbish – but the wax might have stopped a few tiny flea feet clinging to the cloak.

Crazy cures & pointless potions

There were oceans of nutty notions on how to deal with the disease. Daft doctors advised victims to…
• bleed it out using leeches. (Some suckers must have tried it.)
• sweat it out with a hot drink (that's cocoa loco!)
• smoke it out with tobacco fumes. (What – and die of a 'coffin' fit?)
• purge it out. This meant drinking something that made you poo or be sick a lot. The doctors reckoned it would flush all the plague from your body. (What a sick idea.)

Some docs sold 'miracle' potions that they KNEW were useless. They would give free advice – but charge money for their medicine. When victims complained, the docs would say: "My *opinion* is free. My *medicine* is not." Sick people bought their 'cures' – and died anyway. The dastardly docs got rich.

DR KURLEUS CURE-ALL

Spin doctor

Amateur scientist Elias Ashmole hung three spiders around his neck in order to ward off the plague. Did it work? Well, he lived for another 17 years!

MMM– THIS IS ONE BUG WE CAN'T CURE

Evil 18th Century

GOING UP

HOT-AIR BALLOONS
STEAM POWER
MOUSE-FUR EYEBROWS
___
BRITS IN AMERICA
GUILLOTINE BLADES
PIRATE SHIPS

GOING DOWN

After seeing off the Stuarts, the Brits got bashed – by their American colonies. It was a time of crime but things were even more revolting in France.

HALL OF SHAME

BLACKBEARD (C.1680-1718)	PETER THE GREAT (1672-1725)	GEORGE III (1738-1820)	MARY ANTOINETTE (1755-1793)	MAX ROBESPIERRE (1758-1794)
THIS BLACK-HEARTED BULLY WAS ONE OF THE PESKIEST PIRATES EVER TO ROAM THE SEAS. HIS CAREER OF CRUELTY INCLUDED FORCING A PORTUGUESE PRISONER TO EAT HIS OWN NOSE AND LIPS!	PETER WAS A ROTTEN RUSSIAN RULER WHO LIKED TO CURE HIS FRIENDS' TOOTHACHE BY RIPPING THEIR TEETH OUT WITH HIS BARE HANDS! HE ALSO LIKED SERVING GUESTS PIES FILLED WITH LIVE DWARVES.	A CRAZY KING, GEORGE NEVER LISTENED TO ADVICE – WHICH WAS UNFORTUNATE AS HE WAS BASICALLY BONKERS. HE WENT TO WAR AGAINST HIS OWN AMERICAN COLONIES ... AND LOST.	THIS FRENCH QUEEN SPENT FORTUNES ON FROCKS AND FUN WHEN MOST OF HER PEOPLE WERE POOR AND STARVING. THE PEOPLE GOT THEIR REVENGE, THOUGH, AND CHOPPED HER HEAD OFF.	WEEDY BUT WILY, MAX WAS VERY POWERFUL DURING THE FRENCH REVOLUTION. HE HAD THOUSANDS OF INNOCENT PEOPLE SENT TO THE GUILLOTINE JUST BECAUSE HE DIDN'T LIKE THEM.

WORLD'S WORST EXITS

1718 Vicious pirate Blackbeard is caught by Brit Captain Maynard but refuses to surrender. He is shot and stabbed 25 times before Maynard cuts off his head and hangs it from his ship's bowsprit.

1762 A thief steals a sheep. He ties its legs together and places the other end of the rope over his head. Suddenly, the sheep kicks out, pulls the rope tight and strangles the thief.

1789 Starving peasants capture the French finance minister after he tells them to "eat hay". They give him a necklace of nettles, stuff thistles into his hands and fill his mouth with hay. Then they hang him.

WHAT DID HE SAY?

I THINK HE JUST SAID 'HEY'– HAY, GEDDIT?

1793 King Louis XVI's neck was so fat it took French revolutionaries two chops with the guillotine to cut through it.

BEASTLIEST BATTLES

1746 Culloden – Bonnie Prince Charlie invades Britain to put his dad on the throne instead of George II. But George's army is led by the deadly Duke of Cumberland and is much too strong for Charlie's Scottish highlanders. It's an all-out massacre – and Charlie runs away.

1789 Bastille bash – The French are revolting and the first place they attack is the Bastille prison in Paris. After a nasty fight, the measly mob breaks in, frees the prisoners and slaughters the defenders. But it's only the beginning of the bloodshed.

French Frights

Life in 18th-century France was unfair and awful. There had to be a bit of chop and change – so the revolutionaries chopped till they dropped!

40

Mean Queen

King Louis may not have been popular, but his missus, Marie Antoinette, was the person the peasants hated the most!

A fortune teller read Marie's horoscope when she was born. He said little Marie's life would be a disaster. Unfortunately, for Marie that fortune teller was dead right!

When Marie was their queen, the French loathed the way she spent fortunes on frocks when they had no socks. They were disgusted that she played the harp for fun while they starved. (Maybe they just didn't like they way she harped on.)

They even blamed her for all the country's problems and called her "Madame Deficit" (which means Mrs Debt). And the fact that Marie was

Austrian, *not French*, only made her worse as far as they were concerned.

Her hubby, King Louis, didn't exactly help matters. When a nobleman whistled at Marie, the silly king sent him to prison – for 50 years!

QUICK QUEEN QUIZ – TRUE OR FALSE? (Answer on page 61)

Was Marie as bad as teachers say? Test your teacher with this quiz. If they score less than five out of four, they lose their heads...

1. Marie Antoinette was born Maria Antonia. (That's true.) She had six sisters: Maria, Maria, Maria, Maria, Maria ... and Maria.

2. A young man asked Marie to marry him when they were both very young. He grew up to be the famous composer Mozart.

3. One of Marie's best friends always had dogs with her – to help her speak to the spirits of dead people.

4. When the Revolution came, Marie Antoinette worried that someone might break into her room and try to kill her. (That's certainly true.) As a burglar alarm she kept a budgie by her bedside.

41

Bastille Bash

The revolution got going when a mob
attacked the Bastille (say *bast-eel*),
a giant prison in Paris...

The Liberty Tower held a huge gunpowder store, which the mob was desperate to get its hands on. It wanted to start the Revolution with a bang!

Some folk started smashing up buildings, stealing all they could – even roofs. It was a fight on the tiles!

The Bastille was a fierce-looking fortress with a moat. Its eight towers stood 25m high and were linked by thick walls. In the 1700s it was used a prison – from which there was no escape. At least, not until the mob came calling…

OUR SOLDIERS WILL DEFEND US... I HOPE!

HERE, HAVE A BALL!

Nearly 900 men and women stormed the Bastille. Most were poor labourers or craftsmen. It gave them a chance to grab some decent food and wine. (The lower classes raised their glasses!)

WHILE THEY'RE WHINING, I'M WINING!

HEAVE...

The Bastille was defended by just 82 sick soldiers and 32 Swiss Guards. They had one day's food supply left. Hardly a tough enemy!

I DON'T FEEL VERY WELL

Cannons on the battlements couldn't be moved to fire straight down at the mob. So the defenders just used their muskets. They still managed to kill about 80 of the attackers. But this just made the mob madder!

The angry crowds broke through the outer drawbridge so they could cross the moat around the Bastille. You could say the defenders' chances of surviving were 're-moat'!

The defenders were scared and offered to surrender if the mob promised not to hurt them. Did the mob keep its word? Of course it didn't!

KILL THEM ALL, ANYWAY!

OOMPH!

THIS REVOLUTION IS A BLAST!

Many soldiers joined the Revolution – and brought their big guns with them. Cannon can do it!

Streets of Terror

No one was safe from the guillotine. Aristocrats were hunted down and friend snitched on friend. But the poor still starved to death. Rich or poor, everyone was a loser!

Farmers sold animal hoofs and heads to the starving people. It was a 'foot to mouth' existence.

Victims were taken to the guillotine in a 'tumbrel', a type of cart normally used for carrying manure. This was a way of saying "You're no better than poo!"

... something to make your head spin!

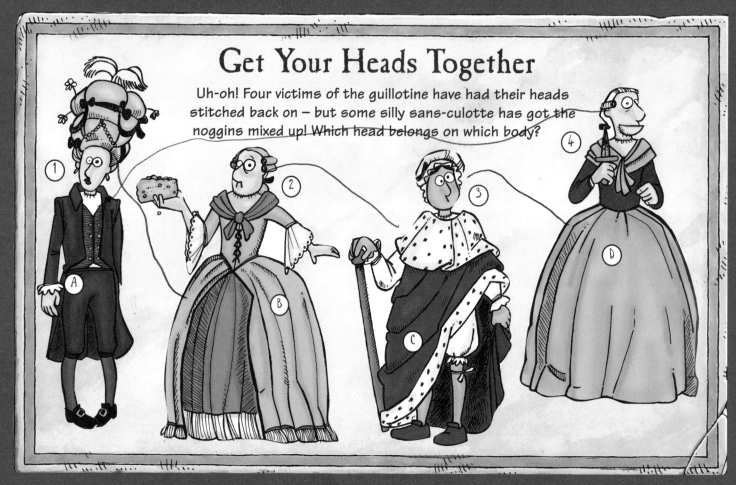

Get Your Heads Together

Uh-oh! Four victims of the guillotine have had their heads stitched back on – but some silly sans-culotte has got the noggins mixed up! Which head belongs on which body?

PRISON PERIL

Can you escape from the Bastille without getting gunned by a governor or sniped at by a sans-culotte?

Answers on page 61

46

GOING UP
BRITISH EMPIRE
THE BRITISH 'BOBBY'
EIFFEL TOWER

AMERICAN INDIANS
TAY BRIDGE
ABRAHAM LINCOLN
NAPOLEON
GOING DOWN

Nasty 19th Century

After they bashed Napoleon, the British Empire got bigger and beastlier. There was a wicked war in the Wild West. The brand new 'Americans' killed the native Americans and each other.

HALL OF SHAME

NAPOLEON BONAPARTE (C.1769-1821)

BARMY BONEY WAS A WAR-A-HOLIC. HE TRIED TO CRUSH RUSSIA, BUT GOT HIS ARMY STUCK IN THE SNOW. 380,000 OF HIS SOLDIERS DISCOVERED THAT THERE WAS NO 'SNOW' WAY HOME AND FROZE TO DEATH.

LORD LUCAN (1800-1888)

THIS RICH BULLY BOUGHT HIS WAY INTO THE ARMY, THEN MADE LIFE A MISERY FOR HIS MEN. HIS BUNGLING AT BALACLAVA CAUSED LOTS OF DEATHS AND EARNED HIM MEDALS AND A PROMOTION!

MARY ANN COTTON (1832-1873)

MARY MURDERED 21 PEOPLE, INCLUDING THREE HUSBANDS AND TWELVE OF HER CHILDREN. SHE SAID THEY DIED OF STOMACH FEVER. THE POLICE OPENED A VICTIM UP AND FOUND POISON INSIDE. MARY HANGED.

GENERAL CUSTER (1839-1876)

THIS FEARLESS FOOL IS NO COWARDLY-CUSTER, BUT WHEN THE US ARMY INVADES AMERICAN INDIAN LAND, CUSTER BLUNDERS. AT LITTLE BIGHORN HIS MEN ARE SLAUGHTERED AND SCALPED!

WYATT EARP (1864-1929)

LEGEND SAYS EARP WAS A FEARLESS LAWMAN WHO KILLED THE BADDIES AT THE 'GUNFIGHT AT THE OK CORRAL'. THE TRUTH IS THIS LIAR AND THIEF REALLY MURDERED HIS UNARMED ENEMIES!

WORLD'S WORST EXITS

1848 Austrian politician Prince Metternich is blamed for the bad state of his country. Revolutionary assassins want to break his Metter-neck. He has a Metter idea and escapes hidden in a laundry basket, Well, he is all washed up after all!

1865 US President Abraham Lincoln has a weird dream about being shot. One week later an assassin shoots him in the back of the head at the theatre. Spooky!

1871 French rebel Charles Delescluze leads the Communard rebellion in Paris. When the Government is beating them, Delescluze stands on a barricade in his best togs. He quickly gets the bullet.

BEASTLIEST BATTLES

1854 Balaclava – The rash Russians invade Turkey so the Brits and the French say "Ha!" and invade Russia. At brutal Balaclava both sides get mashed – mainly the British 'Light Brigade' cavalry, who stupidly charge at the Russian cannons.

1863 Gettysburg – General Lee leads his Rebel soldiers against the Yankees in America's un-Civil war. They meet at gory Gettysburg. Lee launches a suicidal charge at Cemetery Hill. The Yanks get the glory and Lee loses his army.

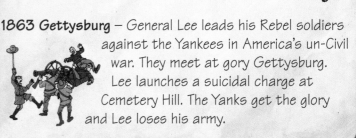

47

How the West was ~~Won~~ Nicked

At the beginning of the nasty 19th century, the new United States of America got rid of the bossy Brits. Now it was time to get rid of the locals who had lived there for 10,000 years. History was about to become really horrible...

THE NEW USA WAS MUCH BIGGER THAN BEFORE. ITS BORDERS STRETCHED FROM THE GREAT LAKES DOWN TO FLORIDA, AND FROM THE ATLANTIC ACROSS TO THE MISSISSIPPI RIVER.

B-B-B-BUT......

AS USUAL NOBODY HAD ASKED THE INDIANS

MANY NEW AMERICANS COULDN'T WAIT TO LEAVE THE CITIES AND TOWNS ON THE EAST COAST AND HEAD WEST. THEY WENT ...

FOR FUN

TO BUY CHEAP LAND AND START NEW LIVES

TO DODGE THE LONG ARM OF THE LAW

AS THE SETTLERS MOVED TOWARDS THE MISSISSIPPI, THEY MET THE LOCALS WHO LIVED THERE. THESE NATIVE AMERICANS WEREN'T KEEN TO SHARE THEIR LANDS...

LUCKILY FOR THE SETTLERS (NOT SO LUCKY FOR THE AMERICAN INDIANS) THE GOVERNMENT HAD ALREADY BOUGHT A LARGE PLOT OF LAND FROM THE FRENCH BETWEEN THE MISSISSIPPI RIVER AND THE ROCKY MOUNTAINS. PRESIDENT JACKSON – OR 'OLD LONG KNIFE' AS THE INDIANS CALLED HIM – CAME UP WITH A PLAN...

THEY COULD CHUCK THEM OVER THE MISSISSIPPI INTO THE WILDS. THE GOVERNMENT POLITELY CALLED THIS 'REMOVAL'.

BETTER TO REMOVE THEM THAN SLAUGHTER THEM!

GEE THANKS!

ALL THE INDIAN TRIBES WERE REMOVED FROM THE LAND EAST OF THE MISSISSIPPI. THE ONES WHO DIDN'T WANT TO GO WERE MASSACRED. THE ONES WHO DID GO DIED OF PNEUMONIA IN THE WINTER AND CHOLERA IN THE SUMMER. THE CHEROKEES, WHO LOST A QUARTER OF THEIR NATION ON THE JOURNEY TO THEIR NEW HOME, CALLED IT THE 'TRAIL OF TEARS'.

MAYBE WE SHOULD CALL THIS THE TRAIL OF BODIES

SO WITH THE INDIANS STASHED AWAY IN THEIR NEW 'HOME', THE AMERICANS DECIDED TO ATTACK THE MEXICANS INSTEAD. WITHIN A COUPLE OF YEARS, THEY HAD 'WON' A MILLION SQUARE MILES OF LAND — CALIFORNIA. THIS TURNED OUT TO BE A BIT OF A WINDFALL.

IN 1848, GOLD WAS DISCOVERED IN CALIFORNIA AND THE GREATEST GOLD RUSH IN THE HISTORY OF THE USA BEGAN. THE PEOPLE RUSHED TO THE REGION TO LOOK FOR GOLD. THESE PROSPECTORS BECAME KNOWN AS THE '49ERS — NOT '48ERS. (WELL, IT TOOK THEM A LONG TIME TO GET THERE.)

CALIFORNIA'S POPULATION GREW AND GREW — FROM 14,000 IN 1848 TO 100,000 IN 1850. THESE GOLD-HUNGRY FOLK WERE A PRETTY LAWLESS BUNCH. SHERIFFS WERE THIN ON THE GROUND, SO THE MINERS TOOK THE LAW INTO THEIR OWN HANDS...

THE CONSTANT STREAM OF SETTLERS HEADING WEST NO LONGER STOPPED AT THE MISSISSIPPI. THEY CARRIED ON AND ON, DRIVING INDIANS FROM THE LANDS THEY HAD ONLY JUST BEEN PROMISED. THE SETTLERS CAME BY THE WAGON-LOAD.

NOTHING STOOD IN THE WAY OF THESE PLUCKY PIONEERS (LEAST OF ALL THE PREVIOUS OCCUPIERS)...

THEY CUT DOWN PINE FORESTS, WHICH HAD PROVIDED FOOD AND SHELTER FOR THE INDIANS, TO MAKE HOUSES, FURNITURE, TOOLS AND FENCES AND SET ABOUT FARMING THE LAND.

THEY FOLLOWED RIVERS AND TRAILS INTO THE MOUNTAIN COUNTRY.

THEY SETTLED IN THE DRY PLAINS, MAKING HOUSES OUT OF EARTH AND DRY BUFFALO DUNG AND DIGGING WELLS FOR WATER.

Wanted: Dead or Alive!

In the new towns of the Wild West the lawmen were lawless and gun-slingers got away with murder.

Some of the Wild West characters were not all they seemed ... in fact, sometimes the lawmen were the worst crooks of all!

Lawless lawmen

Henry Plummer began work in the 1850s when he killed the husband of a woman he fancied.

After a career of killings and robberies, he was elected sheriff of Bannock, Montana in 1863. By then he ran an army of 200 outlaws called 'The Innocents'. Their favourite trick was robbing coaches carrying gold, which had been specially marked with chalk by an accomplice.

He was betrayed by some of his gang in 1864. He asked his townspeople, "You wouldn't hang your own sheriff, would you?" They would – and did! Twenty-four other Innocents were also hanged.

WHY ARE YOU HANGING ME?

COS YOU'RE AN INNOCENT MAN!

Tom Horn was a lawman who became an outlaw. In 1880, he had a job as a detective sent to track down train robbers. Many he simply killed. He always left his calling card – a rock placed under each victim's head.

SO FAR, NO NOOSE IS GOOD NOOSE

By the 1890s Tom had become a self-employed assassin, working for cattle ranchers and killing off their rivals. In 1902, he killed Willie Nickell, the 14-year-old son of a shepherd, as a warning to his father. He was tried and hanged in November 1903. He twisted the rope himself. A photo of him making the rope was taken and proved to be a best-seller!

Vicious vigilantes

A lot of Americans in the 1800s were unhappy with their local lawmen and decided to take the law into their own hands.

In 1851, the citizens of San Francisco set up their own 'Committee of Vigilance', and – unlike your local Neighbourhood Watch (we hope) – gave themselves the power to hold trials and execute!

Their first victim was John Jenkins, who was caught stealing a small safe. He was hanged in the street – and a huge crowd gathered to cheer.

BUT IT WAS ONLY A SMALL SAFE!

DON'T WORRY, WE'RE ONLY USING A SMALL ROPE

HORRIBLE HAPPENINGS

GOOD OLD CHARLIE BROWN

In 1883, in Miles City, Montana, Charlie Brown was a very popular saloon keeper. Troublemaker Bill Rigney came into Charlie's saloon and became very drunk. He began to insult the wife and daughter of a local man. Charlie cracked him over the head and Rigney fell to the floor, dying. Charlie would hang for his murder and the local people didn't want that! So they quickly formed a vigilante committee and lynched the dying Rigney so Charlie couldn't be blamed for killing him!

CAREFUL! WE DON'T WANT HIM TO DIE DEAD

... a cowboy's (and girl's) compendium

NAME THAT PLACE

America – not just the Wild West – has a lot of peculiar place names. Here are ten. Can you spot the one that is NOT the name of a place?

1. Pee Pee (Ohio)
2. Looneyville (Texas)
3. Peculiar (Missouri)
4. Eek (Alaska)

5. Greasy Corner (Arkansas)
6. Dog's Breath (California)
7. Bowlegs (Oklahoma)
8. Bug (Kentucky)
9. Who'd A Thought It (Alabama)
10. Shittim Gulch (Washington)

SALOON SUPER SLEUTH

1. Womenfolk in the wicked Wild West sure had funny names! Can you fill in the blanks with the names in the picture below to come up with the whole name?

1 Cowboy Queen ....
2 Poker ....
3 .... Mustache
4 Jolly ....
5 Diamond Tooth ....

6 Sad Story ....
7 .... the Pig
8 .... the Ton
9 Glass Eye ....
10 The Waddling ....

2. In a temper the town blacksmith has thrown 10 horseshoes around the saloon. Can you find them?
3. Can you find five objects that are really out of place in a wicked Wild West saloon?

Answers on page 61

Fastest Gun in the West?

Was the Wild West's Wyatt Earp a hero or zero? Here's the tall tale...

He was a brave buffalo hunter, ace gunfighter and lawman.

Honest Wyatt brought law and order to Tombstone, Arizona.

With his brothers he took on the evil Clanton Family gang.

The 'Gunfight at the OK Corral' made Tombstone a safe place to live.

The real Wyatt Earp was a liar, horse-thief, stage-coach robber and killer. He was born in Kentucky in 1848.

In the 1870s Wyatt worked as a barman and was a gambler and a cheat – in the book he wrote about his life he claimed that he had been an Indian fighter and buffalo hunter, plus part-time lawman.

SURE... I KILLED HUNDREDS OF INDIANS

He moved from town to town getting jobs as a lawman and getting fired for fighting. Finally Wyatt moved to Dodge, where he worked as a marshal for a few months and arrested a few drunks...

I BRING LAW AND ORDER

WHY DON'T YOU DO SOMETHING USEFUL AND BRING RUM AND SODA

Moving on to Fort Griffin, Wyatt teamed up with gambler and part-time dentist John 'Doc' Holliday and his partner 'Big Nose' Kate Elder. Holliday was dying from tuberculosis and alcoholism but was still feared – he once cut a man's throat during a row over a poker game!

BIG NOSE? DID YOU SAY BIG NOSE? NOBODY CALLS BIG NOSE, BIG NOSE! DO THEY BIG NOSE?

By 1879 Wyatt, four of his bad-news brothers and Holliday had settled in the tough town of Tombstone. They were soon suspected of cattle rustling and stagecoach-robbing, plus cheating at cards. In their spare time they acted as armed bouncers for saloons.

In 1881, a bungled stagecoach robbery left two people dead. No one knows for sure whether the Earps or another gang (the Clantons) had taken part, but it led to the 'Gunfight at the OK Corral' – a row between two rival gangs of thieves over a robbery, not lawmen going after bad men!

Terrible 20th Century

GOING UP
NUCLEAR WEAPONS
MINISKIRTS
CARS
THE USA
BRITISH EMPIRE
HORSE AND CARRIAGES
TOP HATS
ADOLF HITLER
GOING DOWN

A time of amazing new inventions that, sadly, were often used for war and worse! Old empires were on the way out, but new bullies like Hitler and Stalin made the century a misery...

HALL OF SHAME

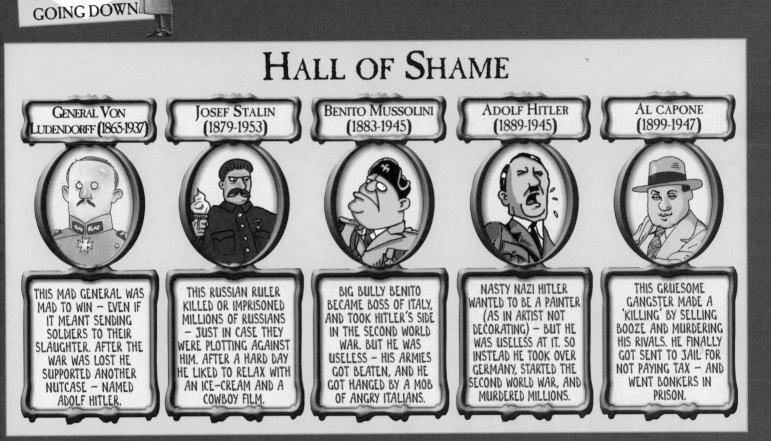

GENERAL VON LUDENDORFF (1865-1937)

THIS MAD GENERAL WAS MAD TO WIN – EVEN IF IT MEANT SENDING SOLDIERS TO THEIR SLAUGHTER. AFTER THE WAR WAS LOST HE SUPPORTED ANOTHER NUTCASE – NAMED ADOLF HITLER.

JOSEF STALIN (1879-1953)

THIS RUSSIAN RULER KILLED OR IMPRISONED MILLIONS OF RUSSIANS – JUST IN CASE THEY WERE PLOTTING AGAINST HIM. AFTER A HARD DAY HE LIKED TO RELAX WITH AN ICE-CREAM AND A COWBOY FILM.

BENITO MUSSOLINI (1883-1945)

BIG BULLY BENITO BECAME BOSS OF ITALY, AND TOOK HITLER'S SIDE IN THE SECOND WORLD WAR. BUT HE WAS USELESS – HIS ARMIES GOT BEATEN, AND HE GOT HANGED BY A MOB OF ANGRY ITALIANS.

ADOLF HITLER (1889-1945)

NASTY NAZI HITLER WANTED TO BE A PAINTER (AS IN ARTIST NOT DECORATING) – BUT HE WAS USELESS AT IT. SO INSTEAD HE TOOK OVER GERMANY, STARTED THE SECOND WORLD WAR, AND MURDERED MILLIONS.

AL CAPONE (1899-1947)

THIS GRUESOME GANGSTER MADE A 'KILLING' BY SELLING BOOZE AND MURDERING HIS RIVALS. HE FINALLY GOT SENT TO JAIL FOR NOT PAYING TAX – AND WENT BONKERS IN PRISON.

WORLD'S WORST EXITS

1916 Rotten Russian Rasputin is hard to kill. Some nobles invite him to a party, then poison him, bash him, shoot him ... and he still survives. Finally they dump him in a frozen river. Nasty!

1918 Bim-Bom the Clown makes fun of the Communists during his circus act. When the secret police jump into the ring and chase him around with guns the audience think it's all part of the act – till they shoot Bim-Bom. Bang!

1929 Two of Al Capone's gangsters are planning to cross him. So big Al invites them to a slap-up dinner... then has them tied to their chairs and beats their brains out with a baseball bat.

1978 The Communist government of Bulgaria thinks Georgi Markov is a troublemaker. One of their agents tracks him down in London and kills him with a poisoned pellet shot from a brolly.

BEASTLIEST BATTLES

1916 The Somme – The British and the French attack the German trenches in one of the muddiest and bloodiest battles of the First World War. But they get massacred by German machine-guns. In the end no one wins, but over a million are killed or wounded in the fighting.

1942 Stalingrad – In the Second World War the Germans storm this city – but the Soviet soldiers and civilians refuse to surrender. There's brutal fighting in streets and sewers. The Soviets win, but nearly two million people get slaughtered.

It's a Nazi Business

The shocking story of how a gang of bullies pushed the world into another planet-sized pickle – and how the good guys beat them back.

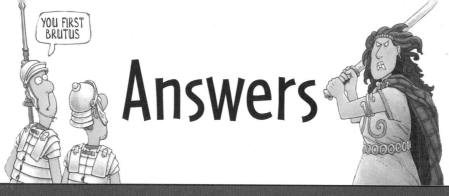

Answers

AWESOME ANCIENT WORLD

Did You Know? page 9 The answer is b. Archaeologists believe they have found the grave of Big Boud under Platform 8 of King's Cross Station.

Army Exam page 10
1. b). 2. a) 3. b). But they often had wives in secret outside the camp. 4. c). But they often barged right down the middle of town streets in their chariots. 5. c). 6. a). Poo! You could use a lump of moss instead, and that could be flushed away. 7. a). 8. c).

Baffling Battle page 12
Latin Break
The odd one out is Mithras – the Roman bull-god.

Odd God Show
They were all real.

Iceni Scene

MONSTROUS MIDDLE AGES

Test Your Metal page 17
1b), 2a), 3b), 4c). Three of four right – Arise, Sir Smarty! Less than three – you're dire, squire!

Brain Tournament page 22
Not at Knight Time
Belong: soap factory, glass factory, water pipes, windmill, clock, vicar, elephant, spectacles, sugar, glass mirror, pillory.

Wrong (because they weren't around yet): hand gun, guillotine, knitting, hymn book, cabbage.

Knight Rules OK
Believe it or not, none of these were real rules. All of those brutal behaviours were OK!

SINISTER 16TH CENTURY
A-Amazing Armada page 28

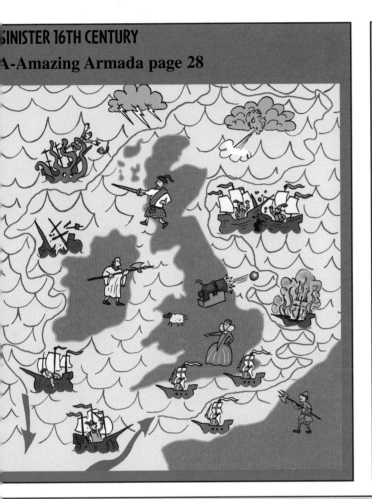

EVIL 18TH CENTURY

**Quick Queen Quiz - True or False?
page 41**
1. True 2. True 3. True 4. False

**Head-spinning Puzzles page 46
Get Your Heads Together**
1b, 2c, 3e, 4a
(spot Robespierre's sore jaw!)

Prison Peril

SCARY 17TH CENTURY
Punishing Puzzles page 33
Puritan Punishments
1 b). Puritans were bad for your bark.
2 a). No snipping on a Sunday.
3 c). That's the last time you'll get 'lead' astray!

4 e). That made an ass out of you.
5 d). Imagine that! No Carol service.

Neck Nick-nack

The answers is b – how tasteless!

NASTY 19TH CENTURY

Cowboy's Compendium pages 52 & 53

Saloon Super Sleuth
1. 1h; 2i; 3j; 4c; 5e; 6a; 7g; 8f;
9b; 10d.
2. Hidden horseshoes are circled
in yellow.
3. Out-of-place items are circled
in red.

Name that place
Number 6 is the only invented one.
The rest all exist.